D1249846

Frank Thomas

Chris W. Sehnert

Published by Abdo & Daughters, 4940 Viking Drive, Suite 622, Edina, Minnesota 55435.

Copyright © 1996 by Abdo Consulting Group, Inc., Pentagon Tower, P.O. Box 36036, Minneapolis, Minnesota 55435 USA. International copyrights reserved in all countries. No part of this book may be reproduced in any form without written permission from the publisher.

Printed in the United States.

Cover Photo credit: Allsport Photos
Interior Photo credits: Wide World Photos

Edited by Bob Italia

Library of Congress Cataloging-in-Publication Data

Sehnert, Chris W.
    Frank Thomas / Chris W. Sehnert.
    p.   cm. -- (M.V.P.)
    Includes index.
    ISBN 1-56239-544-0
    1. Thomas, Frank, 1968---Juvenile literature. 2. Baseball players--United States--biography--juvenile literature. I. Title. II. Series: M.V.P., most valuable players.
    GV865.T45S45 1996
    796.357'092--dc20   95-39960
    [B]   CIP
                                                    AC

Contents

THE MAN IN BLACK

What does a Major League pitcher do when a six-foot five-inch, 257-pound giant of a man wearing black steps up to the plate? When that man is Frank Thomas, the decision is often easy. The pitcher throws four balls out of the strike zone, and lets him *have* first base. "Someday soon, we will see a team intentionally walk Frank with the bases loaded," sports analyst Ken Harrelson told *Sports Illustrated* (September 13, 1993). "And when they do, I will stand up and applaud their intelligence."

Frank Thomas of the Chicago White Sox has played Major League baseball since 1990. He has been the American League's Most Valuable Player two times. His talents have made him one of the most feared hitters in the game today. Though his uniform is black, he is hardly an outlaw.

Frank Thomas of the Chicago White Sox.

LITTLE HURT

Frank Edward Thomas was born May 27, 1968, in Columbus, Georgia. His father, Frank Thomas Sr., worked as a bail bondsman and a part-time deacon for the Baptist church. His mother, Charlie Mae Thomas, was a textile worker. Frank Jr. was the fifth of six children born into the Thomas family. As a boy, he excelled both in school and on the playing field.

At nine years of age, Frank played Pop Warner football. He could knock twelve-year-old players flat on their backs. His coach, Chester Murray, told Frank Sr., "This kid will be a professional athlete. I don't know in what sport. But he will be a professional athlete."

Little League was Frank's first chance to show off his baseball talents. He played outfield, and drew the attention of all spectators. Young Frank learned how to wait for a good pitch, and hit the ball all over the park.

Frank Thomas Sr., is very proud of his son. "I'm not bragging," he said, "but Frank did so well in all sports. And he loved them all." Young Frank was so busy practicing his many skills that he avoided trouble. "I never had to worry about him," his father added. "It didn't matter what time of day or night it was, I knew Frank was at the Boys Club or the playground, somewhere with a ball in his hands."

HIGH SCHOOL

Frank's sports appetite followed him to the dinner table. Grilled chicken was his favorite food. He grew up to be tall and strong. When Frank reached Columbus High School, he was six-feet four-inches tall.

Frank played basketball, football and baseball. He also received honor roll grades for his school work. He was a forward for the basketball team, a tight-end and place kicker for the football team, and a star outfielder for the baseball team.

The Columbus High School baseball team won the Georgia state championship in 1984. Thomas led the way. His batting average was over .400, nearly one hit for every two times at bat! He also developed his home run power. He could hit the ball out of the park in every direction. Frank was voted player of the year in Columbus for 1984, and he still had two years of high school left.

Frank didn't slow down. He sank jump shots for the basketball team, ran over would-be tacklers on the football field, and punished baseballs all the way through high school. He batted .440 his senior year, and was named to Georgia's All-State team.

Professional baseball teams often sign their players to contracts as soon as they finish high school. Most players spend several years playing minor league baseball and only a small percentage are called up to the "big leagues." Frank hoped to sign with a major league team during the 1986 amateur baseball draft. That's when something unexpected happened.

In the 1995 All-Star home run derby, Frank Thomas defeated Cleveland's Albert Bell in the final round.

AUBURN TIGERS

Frank's athletic talents had drawn the attention of Pat Dye, the Auburn University football coach. The Tigers were an excellent football team led by the 1985 Heisman Trophy winner Bo Jackson. Jackson was another star athlete who played both baseball and football. Frank signed with Auburn knowing he could still choose professional baseball if a team drafted him.

To his surprise, no professional baseball team took a chance on Frank. Baseball executives worried he would be a "wasted pick" since he had signed with Auburn. "If I'd been drafted, I would have signed," Frank said later. "I wanted to play baseball."

College was a good experience for Frank, however. He received a football scholarship and also played college baseball. "Playing football for Auburn was a whole new world for me," Frank said. "It made me a man....There, I learned what hard work means." That year, the football Tigers won the Citrus Bowl and finished sixth in the college rankings. Frank played tight-end and caught three passes.

Frank played first base for the Auburn baseball team. He hit .359 his first season. Even more, he led the team in RBIs and set a school record with 21 home runs.

Frank earned a spot on *Baseball America* magazine's freshman All-America team.

In 1987, Frank's football career ended when he was injured during a practice drill. He decided football threatened his future baseball career.

OLYMPIC LETDOWN

Frank's amateur baseball career continued to flourish after his decision to leave the football team. After a successful spring with the Auburn Tigers in 1988, he spent the summer working out with the United States National Baseball Team. These are the players who represent the United States at the Summer Olympics, held once every four years.

Frank played well, batting .339 during the pre-Olympic schedule. He was cut from the roster, however, just before the team was scheduled to fly to South Korea for the Olympic games. After that, he became determined to prove they had made a mistake.

Frank's final year of college baseball was 1989. That year he led the Southeastern College Baseball Conference with the highest batting average.

He set a new career home run record for Auburn with 49. He set another record for most walks in a season with 73.

Frank was voted to the *Sporting News* All-America team and was named the conference's most valuable player. "He was the best we ever had," said Auburn baseball coach, Hal Baird.

DRAFTED AT LAST

The Chicago White Sox general manager, Larry Himes, drafted Frank in June 1989 with the seventh overall pick. Himes was impressed with Frank's hitting ability.

Something else impressed the White Sox. "We also liked the fact that he scored high on our tests in the areas of poise, work habits, and intelligence," Himes said. All of Frank's hard work had paid off!

DOWN ON THE FARM

Frank began his professional baseball career in Sarasota, Florida, in 1989. He played 16 games in the Gulf Coast Rookie League, and another 55 games with the Class A minor league team.

The next spring, the White Sox invited Frank to their spring training. This was his first chance to hit against Major League pitching. Frank dominated the pitchers just as he had done at every other level he had played. He thought he had made the big leagues at last.

But the White Sox wanted Frank to work on his defensive skills as a first baseman. He was sent to Alabama to play for the class Double A Birmingham Barons. The decision disappointed Frank, but he decided to work hard for his new team.

The 1990 season would be a big one for Frank. He played 109 games for the Barons. His batting average was .323. He hit 18 home runs and drove in 71. He was walked a league-leading 112 times. Pitchers didn't like to throw him strikes, and he knew it. For his efforts, Frank was named Baseball America's Minor-League Player of the Year. On August 2, 1990, he received "the call" to join the Chicago White Sox.

*Frank Thomas drives in teammate Steve Sax with a third-inning double
against the Oakland A's.*

WELCOME TO THE SHOW

Frank entered the Major Leagues in the heat of an August pennant race in 1990. The White Sox were chasing the red hot Oakland Athletics for the American League's Western Division title. His first game was a rough one. He went hitless, and Chicago lost to the Milwaukee Brewers.

The next day, Frank got on track. He hit a triple that drove in the winning run. He stayed hot for the rest of the season, but his team never caught Oakland.

Because his call-up came so late in the season, Frank only played in 60 games for the White Sox in 1990. However, he finished the season batting .330, the team's highest batting average. It was the White Sox's highest batting average in 48 years! "Big Frank," as his new teammates called him, had finally arrived.

BIG HURT

Frank had proven he was a Major League ball player. But could he produce for a full season? The answer came in loud and clear.

The Chicago White Sox played 162 games in 1991. Frank played in 158. He had injured his shoulder in spring training, before the regular season had even begun. Yet, he sat out only four games all year, and had surgery to repair the arm after the season.

Six-foot five-inch, 240-pound Frank Thomas has made all of baseball take notice of his enormous talents.

Along the way he posted some tremendous statistics. He finished among the league leaders in nearly every offensive category. He batted .318, he pounded out 32 home runs, and drove in 109 runs.

Pitchers around the league quickly learned what a dangerous hitter Frank was. They walked him more than any player in White Sox history, 138 times. Frank was now considered one of baseball's best hitters. His ability to strike fear in opponents' eyes earned him his new nickname, "The Big Hurt."

DBTH

Baseball fans everywhere now knew of Frank's talents. Sports writers compared him with great Hall of Famers like Ted Williams and Hank Aaron. His popularity could be measured by the high prices offered for his 'rookie' baseball cards.

With all of this attention, Frank remained humble. He pasted the letters "DBTH" above his locker and on his clubhouse slippers. "Don't Believe The Hype" became his new motto. He wanted to improve.

Frank Thomas is considered one
of baseball's best hitters.

THE HITS KEEP COMING

Frank did not let his fans down. He continued to belt the ball or take free passes to first. He reached base more than any other player in baseball in 1992. His batting average was .323, and he was walked a league-leading 122 times. He also led the league with 46 doubles, had 24 home runs and drove in 115.

Frank still wanted to improve. During the off-season, he worked on his defensive skills, by throwing and catching for many hours. He hoped his improved defense would help his team win more games.

Frank Thomas eyes his 20th home run of the season, May 29, 1994, against the Baltimore Orioles.

MVP

The year 1993 was Frank's best season yet. His offensive numbers were among the league's best. He became only the fifth player in baseball history to have three seasons in a row with at least 20 home runs, 100 RBIs, 100 runs, 100 walks and a .300 average. The first four players who had these numbers are considered among the all-time greatest. They are Babe Ruth, Lou Gehrig, Jimmie Foxx and Ted Williams.

Frank Thomas smiles as he rounds third base heading for home after teammate George Bell hit a two-run homer.

What made Frank happiest, though, was that his team won the American League's Western Division Pennant. He was finally going to the playoffs!

The White Sox played the Toronto Blue Jays in the American League Championship Series. Frank played well. He batted .353 in six games. The Sox lost the series, however, and the Blue Jays went on to beat the Atlanta Braves for the World Series Championship.

Frank's great season did not go unrewarded. His 41 home runs were a new White Sox record. At mid-season, he played in his first Major League All-Star game. After the season, every voting member of the Sports Writers Guild elected Frank Thomas the American League's Most Valuable Player for 1993.

Opposite page: *First baseman Frank Thomas is greeted at home plate by teammates after hitting a three-run home run in Yankee Stadium.*

ENCORE

Frank had won the highest individual honor a baseball player can earn for a season. The MVP award is given to the best all around player in each league. What would he do next? How about win the award twice in a row?

That's exactly what he did in 1994. It was a season shortened by a frustrating labor strike. Major League baseball players refused to finish the season in early August because of a money dispute with the owners. With 49 games left to play, Frank already had 38 home runs, 101 RBIs and a .353 batting average.

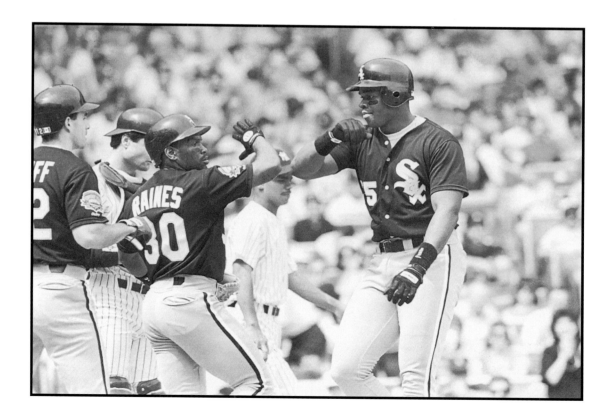

Frank was on a pace to break the all time record for home runs in a season. Roger Maris of the 1961 New York Yankees had hit 61. Because of the strike, Frank would have to wait for another year.

Frank's untouchable numbers gained him his second MVP award in a row. Coincidentally, the last American League player to win two in a row was Roger Maris in 1960 and 1961.

BORN TO HIT

Frank Thomas loves the game of baseball. Only 26 years old, he had already become one of the game's finest players. "I feel like I was born to hit," he said.

Hitting a baseball has been described as the most difficult challenge in all of sports. Even the best batters fail to get a hit two out of three times. Yet, when Frank steps up to the plate, pitchers often walk him. It's better than letting him launch one out of sight.

Opposite page: Frank Thomas
hits a game-winning three-run
home run.

FRANK'S FAMILY

Frank has a successful baseball career, and he's only just begun. He shares his good fortune with the people he loves. He and his wife Elise have two children, Sterling and Sloane.

Frank's younger sister died when he was just ten years old. She had a blood disease called leukemia, and lived only two-and-a-half years. To fight this deadly disease, Frank started the Frank Thomas Charitable Foundation. He donates money he earns from his baseball cards, autographs and personal appearances to the Leukemia Society.

FILL IN THE BLANKS

Frank Thomas has made a habit of doing outstanding things on the baseball diamond. Even in the strike shortened season of 1994, he continued his benchmark streak of home runs, batting average, runs, RBIs and walks. This put him in the select company of Lou Gehrig and Ted Williams, as the only three players to accomplish these numbers in four straight seasons. Even better, Frank did it in his first four full seasons.

At this pace, Frank will rewrite Major League Baseball's record book before he's through playing. He continues to improve with every season. While the World Series Championship remains a goal for him, he has already achieved the highest individual honor in baseball, twice.

Baseball fans from Chicago and around the world recognize Frank Thomas as a special player. His family and friends know him as a special person. He is truly an MVP in every way!

Opposite page: *Frank Thomas answers reporters questions as his son, Sterling, looks on.*

FRANK THOMAS' ADDRESS

You can write to Frank Thomas at the following address:

Frank Thomas
c/o Chicago White Sox
Comiskey Park
333 West 35th Street
Chicago, IL 60616

If you want a response, please enclose a self-addressed, stamped envelope.

GLOSSARY

All-Star: A player who is voted by fans as the best player at his position that year. American and National League All-Stars face-off each summer in the All-Star Game.

Amateur: A person who performs without being paid.

American League: An association of baseball teams which make-up one-half of the Major Leagues.

American League Championship Series: A best of seven game playoff with the winner going to the World Series to face the National League Champions.

Bail bondsman: A person who lends money to post bail.

Bases loaded: A situation in a baseball game when a team has a runner on every base.

Batting average: A baseball statistic calculated by dividing a batter's hits by the number of times at bat.

Contract: A written agreement a player signs when hired by a professional team.

Executive: A person involved in the business dealings of an organization.

Hall of Fame: A memorial for the greatest players of all time.

Heisman Trophy: An award presented each year to the most outstanding college football player.

Home run: A play in baseball where a batter hits the ball over the outfield fence scoring everyone on base as well as themselves.

Intentional walk: A baseball strategy where the manager calls for the pitcher to walk the batter on purpose.

Jump shot: A play in basketball where a player leaps straight up before shooting the ball at the basket.

Major Leagues: The highest ranking association of professional baseball teams in the world, consisting of the American and National Baseball Leagues.

Minor leagues: A system of professional baseball leagues at levels below Major League Baseball.

Olympics: A group of modern international athletic contests held every four years in a different city.

Pennant: A flag which symbolizes the championship of a professional baseball league.

Pitcher: The player on a baseball team who throws the ball for the batter to hit. He stands on a mound and pitches the ball toward the strike zone area above the plate.

Place kicker: The player on a football team who kicks the ball for field goals or on kick-offs.

Plate: The place on a baseball field where a player stands to bat. It is used to determine the width of the strike zone. Forming the point of the diamond shaped field, it is the final goal a baserunner must reach to score a run.

Pop Warner football: An organization of football teams for kids nine to twelve years old.

Professional: A person who is paid for their work.

RBI: A baseball statistic standing for *runs batted in.* A player receives an RBI for each run that scores on their hit.

Rookie: A first-year player, especially in a professional sport.

Scholarship: A grant given to a student to pay for their college tuition.

Spring training: A preseason practice camp for professional baseball players traditionally held in Arizona or Florida.

Statistics: Numbers used to estimate a player's ability in different categories.

Strike zone: The area above the plate and in front of the batter which must be thrown to for a pitch to be called a strike. A pitch out of the strike zone is called a ball.

Tight-end: The player on a football team who lines up on one end of the offensive line. He may provide blocking, go out for passes, or run with the ball on an "end around".

Walk: A play in baseball when a batter receives four pitches out of the strike zone and is allowed to go to first base.

World Series: The championship of Major League Baseball played between the pennant winners from the American and National leagues.

Index